Pebble® Plus

(EXPLORE LIFE CYCLES)

A Butterfly's Life Cycle

by Mary R. Dunn

CAPSTONE PRESS
a capstone imprint

Pebble Plus is published by Capstone Press,
1710 Roe Crest Drive, North Mankato, Minnesota 56003
www.mycapstone.com

Library of Congress Cataloging-in-Publication Data
Library of Congress Cataloging-in-Publication data is available on the Library of Congress website.
ISBN 978-1-5157-7053-4 (library binding)
ISBN 978-1-5157-7059-6 (paperback)
ISBN 978-1-5157-7065-7 (eBook PDF)

Editorial Credits
Anna Butzer, editor; Kyle Grenz, designer
Wanda Winch, media researcher; Kathy McColley, production specialist

Photo Credits
Dreamstime: Rinusbaak, back cover, 19; Shutterstock: Sari ONeal, 17, Cathy Keifer, 7, D.
Longenbaugh, cover, del Monaco, 15, jaimie Tuchman, 9, Kim Howell, 21, Leena Robinson, 11, 13,
Mike Vande Ven Jr., 1, nemlaza, butterfly silhouettes, Perry Correll, 5

Note to Parents and Teachers

The Explore Life Cycles set supports national science standards related to life science. This book
describes and illustrates the life cycle of Monarch butterflies. The images support early readers in
understanding the text. The repetition of words and phrases helps early readers learn new words.
This book also introduces early readers to subject-specific vocabulary words, which are defined in
the Glossary section. Early readers may need assistance to read some words and to use the Table of
Contents, Glossary, Read More, Internet Sites, Critical Thinking Questions, and Index sections
of the book.

Printed and bound in China.
010408F17

Table of Contents

Life in an Egg

A female monarch butterfly floats in the air. She is looking for a special plant. At last she finds a milkweed plant and lays her eggs.

Caterpillars hatch from the eggs in about a week. These little critters eat their way out of the egg using their strong jaws.

Hungry Caterpillars

Hungry caterpillars eat milkweed leaves.

They eat until their skin gets too tight. Pop!

They molt, or shed their old skins.

Underneath is a new, larger skin.

A caterpillar sheds its skin four or
five times. The caterpillar hangs
upside down from a leaf.
It sheds its skin one more time.
The new layer is called a pupa or chrysalis.

11

Inside a Pupa

The pupa hardens as it dries.
Inside the pupa, a caterpillar's
body changes. After about
two weeks, the pupa cracks open.

A butterfly pulls itself out of the pupa.
Its body is wet and folded. Its wings
slowly open and dry in the sun.

15

Life as a Butterfly

All summer the monarch flies

from flower to flower.

It unrolls its long tongue to eat.

The monarch sucks nectar

from the flowers. Yum!

Days get shorter. The weather
gets cooler. Monarch butterflies know
it is time for the long flight south.
They rest in trees along the way.

In spring, the sun warms the butterflies. Most fly north. Butterflies mate and the females lay eggs. Caterpillars hatch and molt. And from a pupa comes a beautiful butterfly!

GLOSSARY

caterpillar—a larva that changes into a butterfly or moth; a caterpillar is the second life stage of a butterfly

chrysalis—the third stage of a butterfly; pupa is another word for chrysalis

hatch—to break out of an egg

jaw—a part of the mouth used to grab, bite, and chew

mate—to join together to produce young; a mate is also the male or female partner of a pair of animals

milkweed—a plant with milky juice and pointed pods; monarch butterflies lay eggs only on milkweed

molt—to shed an outer layer of skin

nectar—a sweet liquid found in many flowers

pupa—a hard casing with an animal inside; the animal is changing from larval stage to the final animal stage

READ MORE

Delano, Marfe Ferguson. *Butterflies.* Explore My World. Washington D.C.: National Geographic Society, 2014.

De la Bedoyere, Camilla. *Caterpillar to Butterfly.* Irvine, CA: QEB Pub., 2016.

Marsh, Laura. *Caterpillar to Butterfly.* Washington, D.C.: National Geographic Children's Books, 2012.

INTERNET SITES

FactHound offers a safe, fun way to find Internet sites related to this book. All of the sites on FactHound have been researched by our staff.

Here's all you do:

Visit *www.facthound.com*

Type in this code: 9781515770534

Check out projects, games and lots more at
www.capstonekids.com

CRITICAL THINKING QUESTIONS

1. What are the stages of a butterfly's life?

2. A caterpillar molts. How many times does it molt before it is full grown?

3. In the glossary, find the word that tells what caterpillars eat.

INDEX